Poems

by

Aminah

Copyright © Aminah Jasmine Rahman 2016

All rights reserved. No part of this publication may be reproduced, stored in a retrieval system or transmitted in any form or by any means, electronic, mechanical, audio, visual or otherwise, without prior written permission of the copyright owner. Nor can it be circulated in any form of binding or cover other than that in which it is published and without similar conditions including this condition being imposed on the subsequent purchaser.

ISBN 978-0-9955093-1-3

Typeset by Bookcraft Ltd

Printed by Lightning Source

Published by:

PERFECT PUBLISHERS LTD

23 Maitland Avenue
Cambridge
CB4 1TA
England

http://www.perfectpublishers.co.uk

Dear Catherine,
Enjoy!

Andrew   March 2021

Spring

Spring, spring is coming soon,
The grass is green and the flowers bloom.
The wind's loud song is heard, day after day,
The leaves break free from the trees, and start to sway.
Flowers dance side to side,
Whilst giving the buzzing bees a rocking ride.
The sky holds blue and so clear,
Ever so perfect, anyone would want to be here!
Spring makes the world a pleasant place,
You see huge smiles on every face.
Flowers grow and birds arrive,
Oh, isn't it amazing to be alive!

Autumn

Descending leaves fall to the ground,
Twirling, twisting, round and round,
Autumn is almost here,
The smell of freshness is ever so near.
The strong gush of wind will blow my silky hair,
Cutting through the cool and chilly air.
Leaves fall like kisses from the wide, blue sky,
Which fall from a place, so high!
The crisp and bitter breeze
Shakes the leaves from the tall and towering trees,
Gold and brown is all that can be seen,
As autumn takes away the appealing green.

Winter

Winter crept through the darkening wood
Passing holly and oak.
He crushed each leaf, never stood
And never a word he spoke.
The streets were like frosted cakes,
The houses were covered in glowing snow,
All cars were covered with delicate snowflakes
As the white began to grow.
The next day the snow disappeared,
It suddenly began to rain
Every speck of white had cleared
And never came back again.

Summer

The sun shines bright, bright as can be,
A perfect time to go to the refreshing sea.
Blue skies hold clear up above
As people gaze at it with great love.
The scorching sun shines right at me,
And sparkles through the gigantic trees.
In winter, when the weather is bleak,
She is often playing hide and seek.
At night, when all is dark, she starts to sleep
Behind the moon till she begins to creep.
She looks upon the earth below
With shimmering eyes and cheeks that glow.

White Moon

The skies above turn a midnight blue,
As the moon starts peeping through.
The clouds move fast, which pass the moon,
Something you never see in the afternoon.
It glows white, white as can be
And the moon is always following me.
The moon is bright, the moon is round,
I see the reflection on the ground.
The circle of ivory gradually begins to disappear
And the sky becomes clear.
The burning sun starts to peek
And is time for the white to play hide and seek.

White Snow

It started to snow, on a winter day,
Everyone could see there was more on its way.
The white fell like kisses from the sky,
Which fell from somewhere ever so high.
I lay in the blanket of snow, as if it was my bed,
Still laying there, turning a bright red.
The eyes of mine looked above,
They fell with pride and great love.
The streets of Cambridge began to glow,
As more of the white started to show.
Ice clutched to the branches of the Tall,
Slowly fading away and began to drool.

The Sun

Dawn arrived; this meant a new start,
I knew we were never to be apart.
I can see the gold peeping through trees,
It makes me blind when it stares at me.
The sun is vibrant, a shining ray of light,
She is always in everyone's sight.
Maybe she needs a really good rest,
From all that shining – she does her best!
Yes, the sun is bright,
But where on Earth does it go at night?
She'll be shining in every place
And always, always in my face.

The Wind

The wind moves in its wonderful ways,
Through the plants it blows and sways.
It takes all the leaves and flies them so high,
Then briefly, he lets go and they fall from the sky.
The wind blows through my long, silky hair,
He was going to knock me over, so I said, "don't you dare!"
Sometimes it tickles the tip of your nose
And sends shivers to the tip of your toes.
Next time you see a plastic bag down your street
And you feel the wind at your feet,
Remember its power and its grace,
The wind can be anywhere and at any place.

Fluffy Clouds

The grey candy floss always surrounds me,
They're lucky, they always seem free.
They form into animals and lovely shapes
This may be weird – trailing capes.
Do they have a mum, a brother?
All I can say is one doesn't look like another.
They are very grey,
But do they just sit there all day?
It's funny because they look like mashed potato,
Most of the time, they're always on the go.
At night, they fade away and the sky is clear,
And I know that they are always near.

The Flood

Buckets of rain poured down one day,
Nothing was going my way.
The water had absolutely no where to go,
All it'd do is grow and grow.
The rain crept into my home, taking all away from me,
My photos, furniture and the one house key.
It was a swimming pool, but only dirty,
This happened soon after the clock struck three thirty.
It soon stopped raining; it dripped from the windows next to me,
It was like the rocking and rapid sea.
It was bitter; I had to clean up,
I just felt like having tea in my favourite cup.

Lightening is Frightening

Rain dropped, heavy indeed,
It all happened at such a fast speed.
A thunderous boom was heard and lightning hit the sky,
If I were outside, I'd probably die.
It was a purple and leafless autumn tree,
He formed millions of different shapes, thin as a key.
The lightning is like fire, the clouds like ash,
It all vanishes in one bright flash.
It's terrifying, the skies above are livid,
It's daunting, especially when you're a kid.

Solar Eclipse

It was all on the news, that an eclipse would return,
It was the first time for me – something new to learn.
We stood outside, the clouds turned grey,
I knew that it was soon on its way.
A few degrees dropped, it suddenly turned cold,
"Don't look at her with a naked eye!" we were told.
The moon crept in, slowly covering the gold,
The moon began to fold.
A sparkling diamond had formed and got smaller as seconds passed by,
It disappeared and I smiled, looking up at the sky.

Rainbow

The rainbow speaks so softly, yet it explains,
"My colours are only shown after sun and rain."
When a rainbow appears, all we do is look up and stare,
She is willing to show her colours everywhere.
She is beautiful; she glistens in the light,
The skies above are always lovely and bright.
Looking towards the clear sky,
The tears of depression gradually dry.
She is like a waterfall, only a lot more fascinating,
She sits there, looks down and begins waiting.
She waits to fade away, and come back another time,
When the rain drops and the sun shines.

Specks of Hail

It was late spring, as I recall,
When pieces from the sky began to fall.
They crashed down and left marks everywhere,
We were told we had to be alert and aware.
They're crystals; they're as sharp as a knife,
Not so sharp that you'd lose your life!
They descended, scraping down our sides,
To stop myself from getting hurt, I'd have to hide.
It came so hard and hit the land,
They ruined all our wonderful things we had planned.
The sun came out and began to shine,
The crystals knew they had passed the line.

The Fog

I stepped outside, looking around,
There was no noise, not one sound.
A vast blanket of grey hung over everyone,
He flew everywhere, covering the sun.
He swooped in and skirted around buildings and trees,
He fluttered, leaving us an icy breeze.
The city was like an old painting – it was painted by an expert hand,
Carrying on, throwing a blanket across the land.
He slowly faded away, making the land clear,
He was always near.
Before he left, he hugged every leg,
And clung onto us, like a clothes peg.

Roars of Thunder

The thunder cracked the sky into two,
A flash, buckets of rain and so the wind blew.
The skies turned purple, and ever so dark.
People getting soaked, the dogs began to bark.
It was like a tree, only without leaves,
It was outrageous, so hard to believe.
Out came a flash; it came out of the blue,
It was like a cartoon, but it was really true.
It was vulgar, too loud to cover my ears,
It was one of our greatest fears.
Petrifying, something I'd not forget,
Whenever I remember, all it brings is sweat.

Earthquake!

Our house started shaking, side to side,
The furniture met in the middle to collide.
The ground rumbled which made things fall,
We were not expecting this at all!
It was horrifying, the ground split into two,
Terrifying; an experience which was new.
All we could hear was piercing screams and cries,
It was like the ground was going to rise.
It was like an erupting volcano, from so long ago,
I lost everything; jewellery, money and my gold
    gizmo.
It was hard to believe; it was like a dream,
All came to ears was that one, deafening scream.

Heatwave

It had been sweltering, for the last few days,
It was great for a charming ice cream sundae.
The waves of the heat rise,
Absolutely no movement, just the buzzing flies.
The breeze dies down,
The sun peeps through the whole town.
You can't sleep on any warm night,
You wonder "when will I leave this plight?"
I'm woken up by the beautiful sun,
"Right," I say, "time to have fun!"
Sometimes I wish for the cold to come back,
You probably want to give me the biggest whack.

Striking Sunset

The day was coming to an end; the skies turned bleak,
And also, a close to a lovely week.
She sparkles over the emerald hill,
She probably says "right, time for me to chill!"
The gold makes me picture the most beautiful dreams,
All I can do is smile and beam.
The fiery orb spreads its magnificent rays of light,
She glitters and twinkles; it is so bright!
The sky turns into a flame – red, orange and yellow,
She waves goodbye and looks below.
The sky melted away into a midnight blue,
Silver sequins appeared – my dream of bliss came true.

The Sunrise

Woken up by a ray of light,
It's seen in the early morning, not at night.
The sun rises and shines like glitter,
She wakes up even when it's cold and bitter.
The sky turns magenta and red, like a pretty rose,
She rises and strikes an amazing pose!
She shines and looks at us below,
She warms us up – head to toe.
I can't even look at her, she is extremely bright.
She is always in everybody's sight.
At night, she goes back to sleep.
Day after day, her doze is always deep.

Glittering Space

I look up from the Earth and I try to see
All the planets that live above me.
I gaze at the glittering and sparkling stars,
I look for Jupiter, Saturn and Mars.
Using a telescope would be the best,
To see Mercury and the rest.
They're thousands of miles away from us,
You can't get there in a train, or a big bus!
You'll need a huge rocket to get that far,
To glide through the sky and pass every star.
Astronauts, comets and a UFO
Space is a place we'd all like to go.

The Beautiful Beach

I lay in the golden grains of sand below the sun,
It was amazing and also fun.
Sand ran between my toes,
The smell of the blue ocean ran to my nose.
The sun shone like a powerful torch,
It burned and it chose to scorch.
Adding flags to the sandcastles is the icing of the cake,
One punch and the castle can break.
The waves whisper, they call me to the sand,
The sea sweeps over my feet from where I stand.
The peace and silence steadily grew,
It was quiet, absolutely no wind flew.

Firework Explosion!

BANG! There goes another one, screaming as she goes,
Fizzle and shriek, there she blows!
A boom, a screech and a very loud pop,
Colourful sparkles, so they did drop.
They lit up the wide sky,
They flew and flew until it was time to die.
They looked like dandelions but only with colour,
Normal dandelions are just blander and duller!
A firework doesn't really look like a rocket,
Remember, don't put a sparkler in your pocket!
Clouds of grey smoke were left in the air,
That's all that was left, to show the fireworks were there.

My Mother

The one person I love the most is my one and only mother,
She is unlike any other.
You've helped me when times were hard,
You've always been there for me, you're my guard.
You've given me all the support I've needed,
I would never have succeeded.
I will never lose my faith in you,
My love for you is always true.
You are the Queen of my heart,
Our love is so strong; we will never part.
I don't know what I'd do if you weren't in my view.
Mother, I love you.

The Bullies

I tried and tried day after day,
To tell the bullies to go away.
They picked on me; I was alone,
No one helped; they left me on my own.
I cried one too many tears,
They were one of my biggest fears.
They pushed me to the floor like a stupid kid,
There was absolutely nothing I did!
They stole everything – my money,
They cackled and thought it was very funny.
I told my teacher and parents the very next day,
I saw deep down in the bullies' face they couldn't take another day.

Grandma

She's kind and I love her very much,
Her smile, her laugh and her lovely touch.
She's always making samosas and giving me a sweet,
It's something everyone loves to eat.
Anything difficult, she always understands,
She is thoughtful, she has magical hands.
She has grey hair and wrinkles on her face,
She always makes my world a happy place.
Her hugs are warm and tight,
There is so much, I could write all night.
There are so many words to express my love,
I could write more than the words written above.

The Football Match

It was a big match; it was time for us to shine,
If we were to win, the trophy would be mine.
I ran across the pitch, waiting for the ball to come to my feet,
As we were playing, it began to sleet.
I ran to the other side where the goalkeeper was waiting,
Our rivals and their crowd were hating.
The football was flying towards the net,
To the other side it was a huge threat.
It smacked the net and I scored!
Our crowd were definitely not bored!
The whistle was blown – everyone wanted more,
It was a great feeling, the crowd began to roar.

Senses of Cambridge

I was walking down the streets of Cambridge, on a miserable day.
I could see the emerald grass.
I could hear people speaking.
I could smell the freshness of the air.
I could feel the warmth coming from Café Nero.
I could taste the divine and gooey fudge running through my mouth, from Fudge Kitchen.
I could see posters hanging off black rails.
I could hear birds chirping and the click of many cameras.
I could smell sweet crepes coming from the white van.
I could feel the sun scorching across my face.
I could taste the delicious chocolate from my hot chocolate.
I could go on forever.

The Best Fish and Chips

There is nothing better than food passing your lips,
Especially when it comes to fish and chips.
The white plate glided across the table so it was in front of me,
I was so glad when it arrived, as I was very hungry.
The smell of freshness ran up my nose,
The ketchup was tangy and was red as a rose.
I cut through the crispy batter of the fish,
I had to say, this was probably my favourite dish!
The grains of salt and the ripe lemon bounced onto the chips,
The chips had a swim in the lovely dips.
I scraped each bit of the plate so it was absolutely clean,
It was probably the best fish and chip shop I had ever been.

A Poem

As you can see, this is a poem.
Whatever you're writing about, you gotta know 'im.
It doesn't always have to rhyme,
People say it eats up your precious time.
It can be a haiku or like a story,
A happy, a tragic or a gory.
It can be long as you want – twelve or four,
Ten or twenty, or even more!
It could be a song, or a rap,
One which involves you to click and clap.
It don't need to make sense to anyone – maybe just
    you,
Is it going to end happily or make you feel blue?

Your Phone

You hold it in its case,
In bed, you drop it and it falls on your face.
You wake up; you're already on your phone,
You carry on, even if someone starts to moan.
You take a selfie whatever the time,
You upload it online and the likes start to climb.
You moan for Wi-Fi before anything else takes place,
It's the end of your world; you need it in such a quick pace.
You're on it all the time, at home, in bed,
Why don't you just rest your head?!
Apparently it's a thumb exercise for you every day,
No matter what happens, your phone will always get its way.

Bake a Cake

Heat the oven to gas mark four,
Once eaten, you know you'll want more!
Start off with a big round bowl,
Cream the butter and sugar, and mix with your soul!
Crack the eggs open and mix again,
Until all is gone and is creamy and plain!
Sift the flour with a large metal spoon,
It shall be going in your heated oven soon!
Pour the mixture into each tin,
Make sure it's all used, don't throw it in the bin!
Once taken out of the oven, leave it to cool,
Cut your slice and eat but remember, try not to drool.

All About Me

I'm Aminah and I'm twelve years old,
I like to wear beautiful silver and gold.
I love poetry and drawing,
I hate science because it is boring.
I love the colour blue and love to act,
Yep, that is a true fact!
I love fun and love a great competition,
I'd like to be an illustrator, not a musician.
I love to cook and love to bake,
I love Ferrero Rocher, Snickers and Flake.
I like swimming, basketball and netball,
A true fact – I ain't very tall.

Poppies

A day about remembering – Remembrance Day,
"Wear me with pride," so the poppies say.
A day to remember the soldiers that died,
If they hadn't had won, we wouldn't be alive.
Row upon row,
The poppies lay and the poppies grow.
We shall never forget those who died
And those who survived.
A poppy represents Remembrance Day,
For those who fought and those who gave their lives away.
So remember all the soldiers on this very day,
Those who fought and those who gave their lives away.

True Friends

True friends are those who help when you're down,
True friends are those who don't make you frown.
True friends come like a gleam of light,
True friends make your life happy and bright.
True friends stick together till the end,
True friends are lovely, they don't offend.
True friends always share,
True friends show pure love and care.
True friends always keep secrets; they never tell,
True friends make sure you're happy and always well.
True friends are always there for you,
True friends are there whenever you're fine or feeling blue.

Heartbreaker

Hearing the most devastating news fills you with pain,
It's something you don't want to go through again.
It hurts; you just don't know what to do,
You try to think it's a lie, but you know it is true.
Millions of tears stream down your cheeks,
Some people go crying on for weeks.
Your whole world just falls apart,
You think how can you mend a broken heart?
You want to run, you want to hide
From all the depression that you were given inside.
It's hard to stay happy; sometimes it takes a while,
But all we want is just to see a beautiful smile.

Bubbles

When a bubble is blown, it flies to the sky,
Sometimes it goes really high!
They're like snowflakes but only they rise,
It makes a little pop sound when it dies.
They're like balloons but only tiny,
But balloons are colourful and sometimes shiny.
When they're blown, they wobble like jelly,
They're perfectly round and they're not shelly.
You just dip your wand and gently blow,
Watch the tiny bubble grow and grow.
They show a beautiful rainbow,
They go on journeys and off they go.

I Didn't Do My Homework

I didn't do my homework sir – I didn't hand it in,
I didn't lose it, or drop it in the bin.
It wasn't eaten by aliens out of space,
Or wiped by my little sister's messy face.
It didn't get eaten by my naughty dog,
I didn't drop it down the bog.
I didn't leave it at my home,
Or in the one land of Rome.
I didn't eat it because I was hungry,
I didn't drop it in the deep blue sea.
My pen did not run out of ink,
Need more excuses ... just need to think.

Biggest Fear

It was my biggest fear; my heart would start to pound,
I would jump and freak if I heard a loud sound.
If I'm really scared, my eyes would drop more than one tear,
I repeat – this was my biggest fear.
I'm petrified, especially when the clock hits midnight,
I pull my duvet over my head so it's very tight.
They always say 'everything will be fine'
I start to worry when the big hand hits nine.
It gives me the shivers and creeps me out,
All I want to do is shriek and shout!
I wish it was something I never came to know,
It's something I don't want to show.

What is Blue?

Blue is the sky on a beautiful summer day – a time to have a cold drink in your hand,
She sleeps over the emerald hills and the glittering sand.
Blue is the winter illness – when we wear woolly jumpers and drink hot tea,
She is the wide ocean, she is the salty sea.
Blue is the colour of a delicious, bright, bubble gum ice lolly,
She's sometimes the rim of a Tesco shopping trolley!
Blue is the rolling river,
In the winter, down our backs, she sends us a shiver.
Blue is the colour of a gigantic, scary shark,
She shows her evil side when it is dark.
There are many different shades of blue,
Different tones, different hues.

The Months

January sometimes brings us the white snow,
Snowballs, we do throw.
February brings us the rain,
We hope for it not to come back again.
March brings us the loud and the shrill,
Flowers grow like daffodils.
April slowly brings in the heat
And daisies scatter around our feet.
May – the days are long,
The wind sings its lovely song.
June is almost everyone's summer dream,
It's all about cold drinks and mouth-watering ice cream!
July sometimes brings the cooling showers,
And The Gold shines on the pretty flowers.
August gradually takes away the bright green,
Autumn is almost what is seen.
September brings the darker days,
Autumn comes using its evil ways.
October introduces the vicious breeze,
We're not happy or pleased!
November brings the bangs and the colourful sparks,
Bonfire night is held in the parks.
December brings the bitter and sleet,
The New Year slowly arrives – everyone is in for a lovely treat.

Lightning Source UK Ltd.
Milton Keynes UK
UKOW07f1445301216
291068UK00007B/21/P